CELEBRATING SEAFOOD

A guide to wonderful dishes, people and places

Acknowledgements

All photographs of Colombia, Denmark, Iceland, Ireland, Scotland, Seattle, Sri Lanka, South Africa and Vietnam copyright © John Angerson, 2005. Cover and page 13 photograph of Mitchell Tonks copyright © Peter Cassidy. Page 52 photograph of Rick Stein copyright © James Murphy. Page 60 photograph of Raymond Blanc copyright © Jean Cazals, recipe reproduced by kind permission from *Foolproof French Cookery*, BBC Books 2002. Page 77 Ruth Rogers' and Rose Gray's recipe reproduced by kind permission from *River Café Cook Book Easy* published by Ebury Press, Random House. Photograph of Ruth Rogers and Rose Gray by Johnnie Shand Kydd. Cover photo of 'Columbia' courtesy of Trident Seafoods.

First published in Great Britain by Simon & Schuster UK Ltd, 2005
A Viacom Company

Simon & Schuster UK Ltd
Africa House 64-68 Kingsway
London
WC2B 6AH

1 3 5 7 9 10 8 6 4 2

Additional recipes by Joy Skipper
Design: Planet Creative, Andy Summers
Food photography: Steve Lee
Food stylist: Wendy Lee
Food photography art direction: Sarah Pilkington
Printed and bound in China

ISBN 0 7432 7570 5

www.youngsbluecrest.com
www.youngsfish.co.uk

In celebrating Young's 200th year, we wanted this book to capture all the things that feed our passion for seafood – the people, places and the many ways to enjoy it. We hope the journey will inspire you to explore further, to eat more and really 'Make Fish the Dish of the Day.'

With thanks to all the friends, colleagues and suppliers who helped us put this book together including Chris Solloway and all our chef contributors. And particular thanks to photographer, John Angerson, who travelled the world to create many of the wonderful images.

Proceeds from this book and its photographs will contribute to Young's continuing work to support sustainable fisheries and the redevelopment of fishing communities in Sri Lanka.

Wynne Griffiths
Chief executive.

Passion for the sea

"defined by its oceans the Earth has always been sustained by its watery depths"

The blue planet. A world of water. Defined by its oceans, the Earth has always been sustained by its watery depths. In turns feared and revered, the seas are a world apart – sometimes serene and beautiful, at others violent and destructive. But from ancient times people have ventured forth on water, relishing the beauty and the adventure of exploring towards an apparently limitless horizon.

Soon the real wealth of the seas became apparent. Mankind started to understand the treasures hidden below the glassy surface, a myriad living creatures and a valuable and renewable resource. All of human cunning, ingenuity and strength were brought to bear to find new ways of exploring further to harvest the fruits of the seas. More seaworthy boats were built, finer nets woven and stronger lines created, as whole new communities, and then industries, grew up around fishing.

Photo In the clear waters of Bantry Bay a rainbow rises over the mussel-collecting boat of Bantry Bay Seafoods

Today, fishing is no less important and Young's is proud to be part of one of the world's oldest and finest industries. We work with people around the globe to find our fish – more than 60 species from 30 countries, from cold northern waters to the azure seas of the tropics. Like our ancestors, we still regard the oceans with awe, knowing the need to protect their rich diversity for future generations.

This book rejoices in fish as the most wonderful, natural, varied and deliciously healthy protein available to mankind the world over. It also marks Young's 200th birthday, when we have many reasons to celebrate: superb seafood, our own heritage and the amazing drive, energy and vision of all the people who work with us – many of them featured in these pages.

So this is an attempt to capture the things which make seafood magical, and those which make us proud of Young's as it is today. We do hope you will enjoy celebrating seafood with us.

Photo A fisherman in Nahtrang, Vietnam – just one of the many countries whose delicious seafood is now readily available in your local supermarket.

Young's History

Two centuries ago, in the same year that Nelson was victorious at the Battle of Trafalgar, another event connected with the sea was taking place. In time, this too would have a significant influence on everyday British life.

Elizabeth (soon to be married to William Young) started selling whitebait on the banks of the Thames at Greenwich in 1805 at the age of 14. She bought fish from the small fishing smacks known as 'bawleys' which were commonplace on the river. The combination through marriage of William's fish-catching skills with Elizabeth's sales ability led to early prosperity for the family business. By 1875, in the hands of sons George and William, Young's was well known for its fish, and was supplying the famous 'Greenwich Whitebait Feasts' – banquets held at the Ship Hotel in Greenwich and attended by many major statesmen of the day, including Asquith and Gladstone.

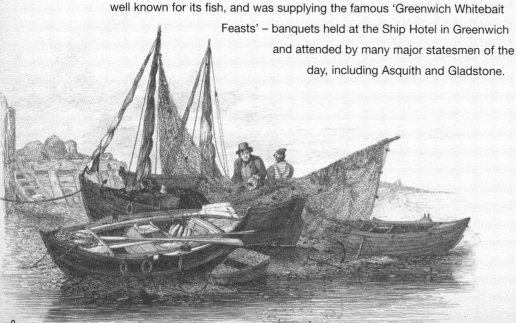

As the 19th century began, Young's was a substantial enterprise. In 1928 it opened its first London office at 40 Royal Mint Street. In the years that followed, Young's became synonymous with great seafood and was responsible for many industry 'firsts' – from inventing potted shrimp and scampi to pioneering frozen food and introducing the first frozen prawns. At one time, Young's even owned its very own fleet of trawlers!

Nowadays, the company that still bears the Young's family name is also still famous for fish. With 200 years of heritage, Young's is one of the UK's best-loved names in food. Perhaps Elizabeth Young would be a little surprised – but probably proud – to know that the business she founded now has a turnover of over half a billion pounds and is one of the world's great seafood companies.

Far left Elizabeth Young started her business buying fish from Thames bawleys; *On this page, left* Later Young's supplied fish to Cabinet ministers at the Greenwich Whitebait Feasts.
Above, clockwise from top Young's was a pioneer in early frozen-food techniques and by the 1950s was using the latest technology in its factories. In 1964, a new headquarters was built in Grimsby. Facing out to the open waters of the Humber, the 10-storey, 135-foot-high Ross House was designed with a curved frontage to resemble a ship's bridge.

New horizons

In 1999 Young's – owned for several decades by large corporations – entered a new era when it joined forces with Bluecrest and became independent again. The complementary skills of these two top names in British fish created a powerful new force in the UK food industry and one with a single mission: 'Make Fish the Dish of the Day!'

Now the company could set about energising the UK seafood market like never before, relaunching the Young's brand with new ideas and a vision to make seafood easier and more accessible for everyone. Since strengthened by many other great seafood names such as Macrae, Young's is building on its heritage and broadening its expertise, helping to shape the UK seafood market for the future. The success of the Young's strategy so far has been to increase the company's turnover by 80% in five years – while it took the Young's brand 195 years to reach sales of £100 million, in just five years this has doubled to reach £200 million in Young's 200th year.

Above Grimsby (top) is the home of Young's. Centre Major new TV advertising launched in 2000. Right Young's staff celebrate the brand's £200M achievement in its 200th year.

As the town's biggest company, Young's is vital to Grimsby, just as Grimsby is vital to Young's. Much work is done with the community and Young's supports many local projects, such as the development of a regional Food Institute and the Grimsby Institute's annual Seafood Championship for student fish-chefs. Young's is also the resolute main sponsor of Grimsby Town Football Club, 'The Mariners'.

Grimsby is home to Young's and where it employs over 3000 people. The times when hundreds of trawlers landed fresh fish at Grimsby dock have gone, but the town is embracing change, and a vibrant new food industry has emerged. In fact, 70% of all UK seafood is now processed in the Humber region.

Complementing Young's in the Humber, the company also employs around 2000 people in Scotland, home to some of the world's finest speciality seafood, such as kippers, scampi and smoked salmon. Young's has been in Annan near Dumfries since the 1940s, producing fine breaded scampi, much sourced from local boats off the West Coast by Young's most remote outpost – at Stornoway in the Hebrides. The company also buys fresh, healthy herring and mackerel from northern ports such as Fraserburgh. When Macrae joined Young's in 2004, it brought superb expertise in chilled seafood, such as the fantastic Spey Valley Smokehouse, where they've been making delicious smoked salmon for over 100 years.

Above Young's is main sponsor of Grimsby Town Football Club and many Young's staff are diehard Mariners fans!. Above right Salmon at the Spey Valley Smokehouse. Right Chief executive, Wynne Griffiths, presents awards to winning students in Grimsby Institute's annual 'Seafood Championship'.

fish for the future

Fish really is the perfect modern protein. Naturally healthy, low in saturated fat and packed with proteins, minerals and vitamins, it's a truly superb food with a tremendous variety of tastes and textures. Everywhere, seafood is promoted as the food of the moment – on TV, in restaurants, by celebrity chefs and in magazines. Even the government advises us to eat more with its 'Two a Week' message.

A powerful new partnership

With 200 years of specialising in fish and only fish, there's not a lot Young's doesn't know about the subject. But, always eager to explore, Young's has teamed up with Mitchell Tonks, award-winning fishmonger, writer, chef and founder of the fantastic 'FishWorks' restaurant chain. Mitch's passion and dedication to seafood is matched only by Young's own, and the combination could prove to be a powerful new force in getting the British to eat more fish.

Centre When young Josh Kesic saw the Young's chefs on TV, he wanted to be one himself! Young's development chef, Serge Nollent, was happy to teach him some of the tricks of the trade. Left The Young's chefs, like Gerry Mahood, delight in finding delicious new ways to enjoy our favourite protein.

Everywhere, more and more chefs are advocating seafood, and many of the best menus feature more fish dishes than anything else. And the Young's team delights in producing delicious ideas to help everyone enjoy more fish, every day. Whether you choose to cook yourself using Young's prawns or prepared fillets or to just pop a healthy and delicious ready meal in the oven, Young's has got the fish for you.

As Young's reached its 200th year, the UK is still only 13th in the league of European fish-eating countries – despite the fact that we have more coastline than the number one consumer, Portugal! So whilst Young's is proud that its recent work has helped push seafood sales to a 28-year high, the company is looking to the future with energy and excitement. There are many more fish in the sea, many new flavours to explore, and many more people who would benefit from eating more fish. Young's intends to help them do it.

Above Young's makes enough fish fingers every year at its Grimsby factory to go round the world twice!
Below Young's 'Seafood Academy' in Grimsby helps fish-counter staff to learn more about fish so they can promote it to everyone.

Top 'Thumbs up' from Young's staff for the drive to eat more fish!
Above HRH The Duke of York was pleased to help Young's celebrate its 200th year with a presentation to commercial director, Jim Cane.
Left Mitchell Tonks is partnering Young's in the drive for inspirational ideas that will make more people eat more fish.

Seafood and the ocean environment

When you consider that fish is one of the last main sources of human food that is wild-caught, you can understand why it is so crucial that we need to properly manage our global fisheries – to ensure the long-term availability of seafood for future generations.

Because modern commercial fishing became so efficient, some of the most popular species started to decline in the 1970s and 1980s, before industry started to take the environmental consequences seriously and apply new conservation measures.

Nowadays, it is accepted that the key to protecting fisheries lies in responsible sourcing policies, encouraging fishermen to harvest in ways that allow the stock naturally to replenish itself, such as by reducing capture of immature fish and actively avoiding some locations. Careful development of aquaculture also helps, with seafood such as salmon, sea bass, prawns and even cod now farmed.

Working closely with fishermen and marine conservation experts, responsible companies like Young's are working hard not just to conserve fish stocks but also to implement all aspects of best environmental practice – avoiding pollution, reducing waste and actively helping in the management of the natural ocean environment.

Young's currently buys more than 60 species from over 30 countries around the world, working in partnership with fishing companies to implement the very highest standards of environmental management. Young's has initiated many new sustainability initiatives, such as its work with Glasgow University to introduce pioneering traceability techniques in Scotland. A trial in Stornoway has already helped scampi fishermen to better understand the Western Isles fishery and adjust their techniques: conserving stocks, improving the quality of the fish they catch for Young's and even increasing their income as a result.

Young's chain of custody code
SGS-NL-MSC-C-0002

Fortunately, there are still plentiful supplies of most species. In Iceland, good management means cod stocks are now increasing year by year, due to changes which the fishing community introduced some years ago. Young's will continue to use its influence in the marketplace to ensure that we can preserve this invaluable natural resource for future generations and to work actively with organisations like the Marine Stewardship Council, which is driving for worldwide seafood sustainability.

Find out more at the Marine Stewardship Council's website (MSC), www.msc.org.

Young's deputy chief executive Mike Parker serves on the board of the MSC.

Northern waters are home to some of our favourite fish. Cod, haddock, salmon, mackerel and sweet coldwater prawns are just some of the species fished and farmed in the cold, clear waters around Scotland and Ireland and still further north to the Baltic and the Arctic Circle.

In the Hebrides, morning turns slate-coloured clouds rosy in the early sunlight. The unpredictable seas here are home to the delicious large 'Dublin Bay' prawns *Nephrops norvegicus* – also known to the French as langoustine and used to make the breaded tails we know as scampi. In Ireland, hemmed in by high mountains is Bantry Bay in County Cork, fed by cascading mountain streams and one of the world's deepest natural bays. This is the ideal location for growing mussels, where clean waters are warmed by the Gulf Stream.

The magical North

Left Aboard the boat Ellen at Rønne in Denmark, veteran fisherman Erling Haunsgaard.
Above Fisherman, Freyr, with a large fresh cod caught in icy Icelandic waters.
Below Colin Nicolson tends his nets in Stornoway harbour.

Salmon
king of fish

Since the early 1990s, the farming of Atlantic salmon has made this delicious fish one of our most popular species. In the UK we now consume over 100,000 tonnes of these fish every year – that's about 10% of the world's total supply!

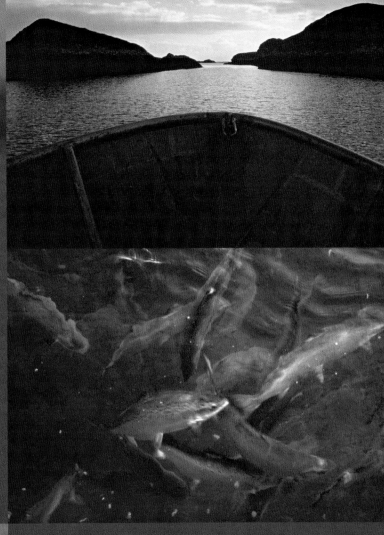

The growing popularity of salmon is good news for our health, too, because it is one of the most easily available oily species – and the many benefits of eating oily fish have been demonstrated in over 5000 scientific studies to date. Young's buys salmon from both Scotland and Norway, from farmers who rear, feed, manage and harvest their salmon paying close attention to the welfare of the fish as well as to the local environment. Best practice means rearing fish that are strong and healthy, in low density cages situated in fast flowing lochs and fjords, where the salmon have to swim hard in deep clean water.

Organic salmon from the Hebrides

Hebrides Harvest has been farming salmon on the Western Isles for nearly 20 years. Based on the Isle of Benbecula, it was founded by Angus 'Scobie' Macmillan, who brought a group of local independent salmon farmers together into a co-operative that became Hebrides Harvest. The company grows salmon on small, owner-managed fish farms under stringent quality conditions around the islands of Harris, Uist and Benbecula.

Left Angus Macmillan of Hebrides Harvest, who supplies Soil Association accredited organic salmon to Young's. These fish are reared in crystal-clear waters at a farm at Sidinish, off the coast of Uist in the Western Isles of Scotland.

Salmon with soy & ginger en papillotte

This is a great way to cook fish – all the flavours are caught inside the parcel and cooked together. You could also prepare this in advance and leave it to chill until you are ready to cook – it's also perfect for a late summer barbecue.

Serves 4

Preparation and cooking time 30 minutes

You will need

4 salmon steaks or fillets
400g (14 oz) pak choi, split in half lengthways
150g (5½ oz) shiitake mushrooms, quartered
2 cloves garlic, thinly sliced
6 cm piece fresh ginger, peeled and julienned

2 red chillies, deseeded and sliced lengthways
6 tbsp soy sauce
juice of 2 limes
50g (2 oz) butter
salt and freshly ground black pepper
4 tbsp fresh coriander leaves

1   Preheat the oven to 220°C/425°F/Gas Mark 7.

2   Roll out two large pieces of foil onto a work surface. Place the split pak choi in the centre of each, followed by the mushrooms. Place the salmon fillets on top, two per parcel.

3   Lift up the foil to cradle the fish and scatter over the garlic, ginger and chilli.

4   Pour in the soy sauce and lime juice and dot the salmon with pieces of butter. Season well.

5   Fold up the foil and pull the edges together to form a sealed parcel. Place on a baking tray and put in the oven for 15 minutes.

6   Remove from the oven and leave to stand for 5 minutes.

7   Serve scattered with fresh coriander leaves.

Alternative Most white fish fillets can also be cooked this way.

Fishfact Salmon is the common name for fish in the *Salmonidae* family, which includes a number of different species native to both the Pacific and Atlantic Oceans, as well as freshwater and sea trout. The most popular salmon eaten in the UK is farmed Atlantic salmon, from both Scotland and Norway.

Producing smoked salmon the traditional way

Visit the Spey Valley Smokehouse near Grantown-on-Spey and warm, wood-scented smoke will lazily curl around you. And within the gloom you'll spy the copper gleam of the finest salmon hanging in neat rows. Established back in 1888, the smokehouse is part of Young's operation in Scotland and is still highly respected today for its traditional production techniques and superb quality.

The salmon is first cured in trays with a layer of pure sea-salt crystals mixed with molasses sugar. It is then washed and hung in the traditional way in the cold kiln, where it is allowed to dry for two hours. Fires are then set in kiln boxes.

Left Jack Wilkinson – smoked salmon expert and manager of the smokehouse at Spey Valley, Scotland.

A wide variety of locally sourced woods are used, each of which can impart a different flavour to the salmon. Some of the fuels used at Spey Valley include oak chip from used whisky casks, birch, juniper and spruce woods, as well as local highland heather, gorse and peat. Once the fires are going, water is sprinkled over the flames to encourage the slow burning process. The smoke is drawn from the kiln box into the kiln, where it circulates around the salmon sides. The smoking process takes up to 24 hours, imparting Spey Valley's distinctive flavour to the salmon. After that, the salmon is moved to the 'post smoke chill' where it stays for up to 48 hours, enhancing flavour and quality.

After smoking is complete, the fillets are carefully trimmed and boned by hand, before being sliced and packaged for sale at supermarkets around the country, to local visitors and by mail order.

Above New product development manager of Macrae, Marilyn Rattray, knows more about smoked salmon than just about anyone else! Here she experiments with some of what she calls her 'funky smokes' – finding delicious natural woods and herbs to create new flavours for smoked salmon at the Spey Smokehouse in Scotland. Centre Alaskan salmon hang in the Spey Valley Smokehouse after hours of smoking.

One man's story

In Stornoway in the Hebrides, Young's has for many years bought freshly caught scampi from the local fishermen. These delicious large cold water prawns are also known as langoustine or Dublin Bay prawns. Larger ones are still sold as whole langoustine to the French or English restaurant market, where they are highly prized.

The scampi are processed locally at Young's factory at Goat Island in Stornoway, where the manager is John Nicolson.

John is a softly spoken Hebridean who speaks Gaelic with his friends and family. He left the islands at the age of 16 and joined the Merchant Navy. After achieving his Master Mariner certificate at 26, he was promoted to his first command after the ship he was serving on suffered a 35 degree list when its cargo shifted in hurricane-force winds. Since the captain had suffered a heart attack, it was left to John to nurse the ship through mountainous seas for 48 hours before he could make safe landfall at Cork!

After 20 years in the Merchant Navy, John came home for a new challenge and started work in the fish industry. He ran a trawler successfully for a few years and then set up the Stornoway Fisherman's Co-Op in 1978. This organisation has since become integral to the local fishing community, providing services and support for all the boat owners.

John moved into seafood processing in 1985 and worked at Goat Island under one of its previous owners. After a spell in salmon farming, he returned to manage the Goat Island factory in 1989.

Due in no small way to John's close ties with the local fishing community, Young's has forged strong working relationships in Stornoway and now buys about 80% of all the prawns landed there. Recently, John and the Young's scampi team have been particularly busy working with several of the boats in Stornoway that have run trials of a pioneering traceability project called Young's Trace designed to improve the quality and sustainability of scampi in the Western Isles.

Left John Nicolson.

Hebridean prawns in whisky cream

JOHN NICOLSON

Serves 5 or 6 as a starter, or 4 as a light lunch

Preparation and cooking time **12 minutes**

You will need

50g (2 oz) butter
1 small onion, finely chopped
350g (12 oz) fresh Hebridean prawns (scampi) shelled
2 tbsp Islay malt whisky
150ml (5 fl oz) double cream
50g (2 oz) grated cheese
chopped parsley to garnish
Freshly ground salt and pepper

1 Use half the butter to grease 4–6 ramekin dishes, depending on size.

2 Melt the remaining butter in a pan and fry the onion until soft.

3 Add the prawns and heat through, then add the malt whisky and cook for a further 2 minutes.

4 Stir in the cream and then remove the mixture from the heat before it reaches boiling.

5 Season to taste and pour into the ramekin dishes, top with the grated cheese and brown under a hot grill.

6 Serve immediately, garnished with chopped parsley.

The combination of malt whisky and cream makes a wonderfully rich sauce. Serve with crusty bread.

Fishfact
Surprisingly, in value terms, scampi is the UK's most important fish catch.

e image
men prepare the
of the Ocean Gain
to setting sail.
e Scampi are
d into Young's
at Stornoway
ur.

Moules marinières

Sorting the mussels by hand at Bantry Bay Seafoods in Cork.

Bantry Bay Seafoods is one of Ireland's leading seafood suppliers. Its mussels are grown on ropes in the bay, harvested by hand and then carefully graded and cooked, to ensure only mussels of the highest quality are packed and sent to Young's.

Serves 4

Preparation and cooking time 15 minutes

You will need

2kg (4$^{1}/_{2}$ lb) fresh mussels
40g (1$^{1}/_{2}$ oz) butter
2 onions, peeled and chopped
2 cloves garlic, peeled and chopped
250ml (8 fl oz) white wine
150ml ($^{1}/_{4}$ pt) water
4 tbsp freshly chopped parsley
seasoning

1   Clean the mussels thoroughly and pull off any beards.

2   Melt half the butter in a lidded pan large enough to take all the mussels.

3   Fry the onion and garlic for 1 minute then add the wine and water.

4   Bring the liquid to the boil and tip in the mussels. Cook for only a few minutes, shaking the pan a couple of times, until all the mussels are open – discard any that are not. Using a slotted spoon remove the mussels and keep warm.

5   Bring the liquid to the boil and reduce for 2–3 minutes. Whisk in the remaining butter and season.

6   Sprinkle in the parsley and pour over the mussels.

7   Serve with crusty bread to mop up the wonderful juices.

Fishtip Preparing mussels

Scrape away any barnacles with the back of a round-bladed knife. Pull away the beard. Scrub the shells well and ensure they are tightly closed or will close when tapped.

Smoked mackerel, avocado & cashew nut salad

Serves 4

Preparation and cooking time **20 minutes**

You will need

400 g (14 oz) smoked mackerel (peppered can be used, if preferred)
200 g (7 oz) watercress
2 ripe avocados, peeled, stoned and diced
20 cherry tomatoes, halved
1/2 cucumber, cut into chunks
100 g (3 1/2 oz) roasted cashew nuts, lightly crushed
2 tbsp sherry vinegar
6 tbsp extra virgin olive oil

1　Preheat the oven to 180°C/350°F/Gas Mark 4

2　Place the smoked mackerel skin-side down on a baking tray and place in the oven for 10–12 minutes while you prepare the other ingredients.

3　Place the watercress, avocados, tomatoes, cucumber and cashew nuts into a salad bowl.

4　Combine the vinegar and olive oil and pour over the salad. Toss gently.

5　Divide the salad between four plates. Remove the mackerel from the oven and peel off the skin. Flake the fish into large pieces and scatter over the salad.

This may seem like a rich salad, but all the fats in this are good ones, especially those in the mackerel!

Fishfact Oily fish is rich in Omega 3 – a 'wonder substance' for the many benefits it can bring for our health. In fact, the government recommends that everyone should eat at least two portions of fish a week, one of which should be oily. The richest natural sources of Omega 3 are fish such as mackerel, salmon and herring.

Fillet of turbot with ginger hollandaise

Serves 4

Preparation and cooking time 30 minutes

You will need

2 egg yolks
2 tbsp water
220g (7 1/2 oz) unsalted butter,
   melted
juice of 1/2 lemon
2 1/2 cm fresh ginger, grated
salt and freshly ground black pepper

2 tbsp olive oil
4 fillets of turbot (approx 200g each)

1 To make the hollandaise, put the egg yolks and water into a glass bowl set over a pan of simmering water, making sure the base of the bowl is not touching the water.

2 Whisk until the mixture has doubled in size and is thick and creamy.

3 Remove the bowl from the heat and gradually whisk in the melted butter to thicken more.

4 Whisk in the lemon juice and ginger and a little salt. Keep warm over a pan of warm water whilst you cook the fish.

5 Heat the olive oil in a frying pan and cook the turbot for 4–5 minutes on each side, until golden and cooked.

6 Serve the turbot with new potatoes and fresh green beans and lots of buttery hollandaise.

Found in the North Sea, turbot is a big fish from the flat fish family. Sold in steaks or fillets, it has an exquisite flavour and is best served simply, with hollandaise – this is a classic dish with a twist.

Fishfact Turbot are bottom-dwelling, carnivorous flat fish and are found in European waters from the far north of Scotland to the Mediterranean.

Northern lights

Icicles, snow, sunlit glaciers – a cold northern world where seafood is plentiful and fishermen brave and hardy. Cod and haddock are still mainstay species here, and good management practice in the Baltic, Barents Sea and Arctic Ocean is ensuring long-term sustainability for these fisheries.

Traditionally, cod and haddock are the UK's favourite fish – and still account for nearly 30% of all the seafood we eat. Young's has close working relationships with a number of suppliers who fish carefully in these cold northern waters and make it possible for us still to enjoy the delicious wild-caught fish that we love so much.

In the Baltic, one of Young's leading suppliers of cod is Espersens. Based in Rønne, in Denmark, it was founded in 1937 and is one of the region's biggest fish companies, with a proud history and a strong record in fisheries management.

Left Icicles on the boats in Bornholm, Denmark.
Above Freshly caught cod is packed in ice at Bornholm harbour.
Below Fish and chips remains a traditional British favourite – around one billion fish and chip meals are eaten in the UK every year, including the best-selling cook at home brand Young's 'Chip Shop'.

Cold-water prawns from the Arctic

Long favoured for the traditional British prawn cocktail, the cold-water prawns (or shrimp) of the *Pandalus* species have a delicious sweet taste. They are fished from the clean, cold seas of the North Atlantic Ocean in and around the Arctic Circle and are one of the most important commercial shellfish species in the world. In Iceland, one of Young's major suppliers is the Fisk Seafood Group, based in Grundarfjordur and Holmavik. With over 20 years in business, it is one of the region's most experienced shrimp companies.

Large image The surreal landscape of Grundarfjordur. *Top right* Ívar Pálsson checks the quality of the fresh caught cold-water prawns off the coast of Iceland. *Bottom right* Harbour-worker Sigmar Fridbjornsson in the thick snow of Grundarfjordur harbour.

Fish pie

Serves 4

Preparation and cooking time 1 hour

You will need

4 eggs	4 tbsp crème fraiche
175g (6 oz) cod fillet	250g (9 oz) prawns
175g (6 oz) smoked haddock	1 1/2 tbsp freshly chopped dill
400ml (14 fl oz) milk	900g (2 lb) potatoes, peeled and chopped
65g (2 1/2 oz) butter	1 tsp Dijon mustard
2 sticks celery, sliced	65g (2 1/2 oz) cheddar cheese, grated
3 tbsp flour	salt and freshly ground black pepper

1 Preheat the oven to 200°C/400°F/Gas Mark 6.

2 Put the eggs in a pan and bring to the boil – boil for 8 minutes and then rinse under cold water to prevent colouration. Peel and leave to one side.

3 Place the cod and haddock in a large pan and cover with the milk. Season with pepper and slowly bring to the boil. Remove from the heat and leave for 5 minutes. Drain the fish, reserving the milk. Flake the fish into big chunks and remove the skin.

4 Melt the butter in the same pan and sauté the celery until starting to soften. Stir in the flour to make a roux, cook for a couple of minutes and then stir in the reserved milk. When the sauce thickens, cook for another 2 minutes.

5 Stir in 2 tbsp of the crème fraiche, prawns, dill and the reserved fish, trying not to break up the chunks too much. Gently stir in the eggs that have been cut into quarters. Check for seasoning and then pour the mixture into a large ovenproof dish.

6 Bring the potatoes to the boil in salted water. When they are tender, drain and mash with the remaining crème fraiche and mustard. Finally whisk the grated cheese in with a fork and season well. Spoon the potato over the fish mixture and, using a fork, spread it over the filling.

7 Bake in the oven for 25–30 minutes, until the top is golden.

Alternative: The great thing about fish pie is that practically any fish can be used – the chunkier varieties are best. Mix and match – you can even use three varieties in one pie and any selection of seafood: mussels, squid etc., the choice is endless!

Fishfact

Haddock with creamed leeks, runner beans & chervil

MITCHELL TONKS

Preparation and cooking time 30 minutes

You will need

2 medium leeks
50g (1³/₄ oz) runner beans
200ml (7 fl oz) double cream
sea salt and freshly ground black
  pepper

1 tsp English mustard
2 tbsp vegetable oil
4 x 75g haddock fillets
a small handful of fresh chervil,
  chopped

1   Remove the roots from the leeks and cut off the tops. Split the leeks in half and chop
     as finely as possible, then wash to remove any mud or dirt.

2   Prepare the runner beans using a bean slicer or just remove the strings from the side
     and chop them into fine slices on a slant across the bean.

3   Place the leeks and beans into an empty saucepan, stir them together and cover.
     Place them over a gentle heat, checking every minute or so and giving them a stir –
     you will be surprised how much liquid will come out of the leeks, and they won't burn.
     Continue to stir until the leeks and runner beans have softened, which will take 7–8
     minutes.

4   Strain the liquid off and return the leeks and beans to the pan with the cream, a pinch
     of salt and the mustard. Add some freshly ground black pepper (I like lots) and
     continue to cook for a few more minutes. You can cook these vegetables in advance –
     they are easy to reheat.

5   Preheat the oven to its maximum temperature. Add the vegetable oil to a hot frying
     pan. Season the fish with a little sea salt and fry flesh-side down until golden for 5–6
     minutes then put the pan (or transfer to a roasting tray) into the preheated oven for a
     further 3–4 minutes.

6   Remove from the oven, add the chervil to the leeks, place a spoonful of the leek
     mixture on each plate and place the fish on top.

Mitchell Tonks

Mitchell Tonks is founder and
oversees the running of the
FishWorks chain of fishmongers
and seafood cafés. FishWorks
was named 'Best Fish Restaurant
2005' in the ITV London restaurant
awards. Mitch has won
widespread acclaim for his books
and has appeared on a host of
food programmes. He is currently
working alongside Young's on new
fish inspirations and appears on-
pack on some of Young's most
exciting new chilled recipes.

Under an azure sky

Clear blue waters, an azure sky and dazzling sunlight. The rocky coast of Greece is traditionally a fishing paradise, where tight-knit communities rely on the sea and work hard together. Here too is a new aspect of fishing, the farming of delicious, top quality sea bass.

Photo In Greece, Mohamet Ali loads freshly harvested sea bass into ice tanks before they are flown by air to the UK.

Sea Bass from Greece

Once a fish that few British people ate, sea bass is rapidly becoming one of our most popular species. Young's buys sea bass from around the world, but a major supplier is Selonda in Greece, which farms high quality sea bass just offshore. Harvested and then immediately packed in protective ice, these bass are then air-freighted the same day ensuring that Young's receives only the freshest quality fish.

Large image Sea bass farmed off the coast of Saronikos, mainland Greece.
Above Net-mender Maria Kletta.
Right Sea-bass worker Prem Singh.
Top right Santiago Gonzalez and Prem Singh throw the sea-bass into ice tanks ready to travel back to the processing factory.

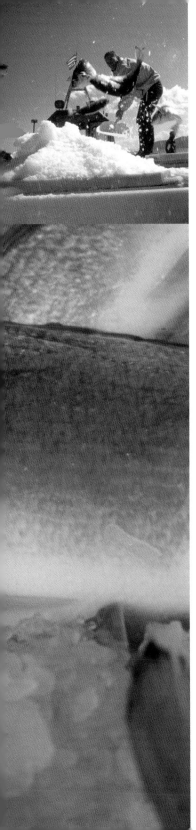

Fillet of sea bass with beetroot pesto

Serves 4

Preparation and cooking time 20 minutes

You will need

4 fillets of sea bass
2 tbsp olive oil
salt and freshly ground
   black pepper
salad leaves, to serve

and for the pesto

2 handfuls of basil leaves
2 medium beetroot, cooked
   and peeled
85g (3 oz) Parmesan, grated
40g (1½ oz) pine nuts,
   toasted
100ml (3½ fl oz) extra virgin
   olive oil

1   First make the pesto. Place all the ingredients in a food processor or blender and whizz together, adding more olive oil if you require a smoother consistency.

2   Heat the remaining 2 tablespoons of olive oil in a frying pan and season the sea bass fillets with salt and pepper. When the oil is hot, add the fillets and cook, skin-side down, for 8–9 minutes, then turn over and cook for a further 1–2 minutes on the other side, until golden.

3   Serve the fillets on a bed of salad leaves with the pesto drizzled around.

A bit of a twist on the normal pesto – adding beetroot gives a real sweetness to the sauce.

Fishfact

In Britain, most wild sea bass are caught in the southern half of the country, mostly by hand lines.

Mediterranean fish stew

Serves 4

Preparation and cooking time **30 minutes**

You will need

1 large fennel bulb
2 tbsp olive oil
1 garlic clove, chopped
200ml (7 fl oz) dry white wine
300ml ($^1/_2$ pt) fish stock
2 x 400g can chopped tomatoes
pinch of sugar

250g (9 oz) cherry tomatoes, halved
450g (1 lb) monkfish fillet, cut into
   bite-size chunks
12 large raw tiger prawns
12 mussels, cleaned
freshly chopped parsley to serve
salt and freshly ground black pepper

1   Remove the feathery tops from the fennel, roughly chop and set aside. Roughly chop the remaining fennel.

2   Heat the olive oil in a frying pan and fry the fennel for 5 minutes. Add the garlic and fry for a further minute.

3   Stir in the wine, stock, canned tomatoes and sugar and bring to the boil. Simmer for 5 minutes before adding the cherry tomatoes and seasoning and simmering for a further 3 minutes.

4   Add the monkfish, prawns and mussels, bring back to a simmer, cover and cook for 5–7 minutes or until all the mussel shells have opened and the fish is cooked (discard any mussels that remain closed).

5   Serve with freshly chopped parsley and chunks of crusty bread for mopping up the juices.

Fishfact You will rarely see a whole monkfish for sale, not only are they extremely ugly fish but the head represents over 50% of the body weight and has little food value except for stock!

Bouillabaisse moderne with spaghetti of provençale vegetables

GERMAIN SCHWAB

Germain Schwab

Germain Schwab is the proprietor of the renowned Winteringham Fields restaurant in Lincolnshire. Amongst many accolades, he is the holder of two Michelin stars and has won many awards including Restaurant of the Year and Egon Ronay Guide Kitchen of the Year.

Germain is pictured here working with competitors at the annual Seafood Championship for student fish chefs, sponsored each year by Young's and hosted by Grimsby Institute.

You will need

500g (1 lb) red mullet, filleted, scaled and pin-boned
300g (10½ oz) fillet sea bass
1 baby monkfish tail
2 tbsp olive oil
1 stick celery
1 medium leek
1 white onion
5 sprigs thyme
5 peppercorns
2 juniper berries
300ml (½ pt) white wine
1 tbsp tomato purée
salt and freshly ground black pepper

for the butter squares

125g (4½ oz) butter, softened
A few saffron strands
3 cloves garlic
1 sheet filo pastry
75g (2¾ oz) warm mashed potato
1 egg, beaten
oil for deep frying

for the spaghetti of vegetables

1 medium courgette
2 large carrots
1 bulb fennel
lemon juice

12 live mussels, cleaned
12 pallourde clams, cleaned
4 whole tiger prawns

1   Fillet all the fish, saving the bones, and portion each fish into four. Peel and de-vein the prawns.

2   Heat the olive oil in a pan and sweat off the celery, leek, onion, 1 carrot and half the fennel.

3   Add the saved bones, thyme (reserving some), peppercorns, juniper berries, white wine and the tomato purée. Bring to the boil and simmer for 35–45 minutes, strain through a fine sieve and reduce to sauce consistency. Reserve until ready to serve.

4   Blitz the softened butter with the saffron and three garlic cloves, season well, then add the mashed potato and season again. Chill then cut into 2cm cubes. Wrap the butter mixture in filo, sealing well with egg wash.

5   Use the remaining fennel, carrot and the courgette for the vegetable spaghetti by cutting into a fine julienne. Blanch separately until just cooked, then refresh in cold water.

6   To serve, pan-fry the red mullet, sea bass and monkfish, steam the mussels and clams until they open, and when these are nearly cooked fry the prawns.

7   Sauté the spaghetti quickly, season well with salt, pepper, reserved thyme and a little lemon juice.

8   Reheat the sauce.

9   Deep fry the filo pastry squares for 1–2 minutes, until golden.

10   Spoon the vegetables into a ring mould, compact down and turn out onto a plate. Arrange the fish on top as well as the filo-covered squares. Spoon the sauce around and arrange the clams and mussels.

Fishfact Bouillabaisse is the classic Provençale fish stew, a speciality particularly of Marseille, but made the length of the French Mediterranean coast. The word bouillabaisse is a French version of provencal bouiabaisso, literally meaning 'boil and settle'.

African adventures

As the new day's sun emerges from a vast horizon the docks are bathed in an unearthly light. Cormorants perch on the jetty, stretching out their wings to dry, and seagulls wheel low to the water's edge. A lone worker hoses down the quay – a new African day has begun.

Large image Cleaning the docks at sunrise, Saldanha South Africa.
Bottom left Young's Seafood's hake supplier in South Africa, Sea Harvest, has set up an independent laundry now run by locals that not only provides a service for the Sea Harvest workers but also takes on contracts from other local businesses.
Left James Baker, skipper of the Harvest Krotoa. Above Victoria Blackwell in front of the Harvest Krotoa.

South African hake

Hake is a well-flavoured white fish that is becoming increasingly popular in the UK as an alternative to cod or haddock. In South Africa, Young's buys hake from Sea Harvest, a progressive fishing company that was also named as one of South Africa's 'Best Companies to Work for' in 2004. Based in Saldanha, on the west coast, Sea Harvest operates a fleet of 15 trawlers and processing facilities. It is one of South Africa's foremost fishing companies, leading the drive for best practice in the industry. As well as being delicious, South African Cape Hake is a good environmental choice, since the Marine Stewardship Council certified the fishery as sustainable in 2004.

Above Worker poses for the camera during a break from unloading the catch on the docks, Saldanha, South Africa.
Right Supervisor inspects the freshly caught hake on the docks, Saldanha, South Africa.

Steamed hake with pak choi

Serves 4

**Preparation and cooking time 20 minutes
plus 1 hour marinating**

You will need

4 hake loins, weighing approx. 150 g (5½ oz) each
4 pak choi, halved lengthways

for the marinade

1 stalk lemon grass, chopped and
  lightly crushed
2 kaffir lime leaves, crumbled
2 tbsp soy sauce
1 clove garlic, crushed
2cm piece fresh ginger, peeled and
  shredded
½ red chilli, deseeded and finely
  chopped (optional)
juice of 1 lime
1 tbsp olive oil

and for the Thai dressing

2 tbsp lime juice
3 tbsp olive oil
1 tsp sesame oil
1 tbsp soy sauce
½ tsp brown sugar
5mm piece fresh ginger, peeled and finely
  chopped
1 small clove garlic, crushed
½ red chilli, deseeded and finely
  chopped (optional)
1 tbsp chopped fresh basil
1 tbsp chopped fresh coriander

1 In a shallow, non-metallic bowl, mix together all the marinade ingredients, then add the hake.
   Leave the fish to marinate for an hour, turning it after 30 minutes to make sure all of it is coated
   in the marinade.

2 Whisk together the dressing ingredients and leave to infuse.

3 Place a steamer over the heat and add the pak choi. Place the fish on top, cover, and steam
   for 5–7 minutes, depending on the thickness of the fish.

4 Serve the fish on top of the pak choi and spoon over the dressing. Some steamed rice would
   also be good for soaking up the wonderful juices.

Fishfact
Did you know that there are at least 14 species of hake? *Carpensis*, often referred to as Cape Hake, is one of the most highly valued.

49

Above In Vietnam, lines of women workers prepare tropical prawns for export in the space-age sterile environment at the factory of Young's supplier, the Truc Anh Corporation. *Below* Nguyen Van Hoang checks the quality of growing prawns in the ponds at one of Truc Anh's farms. *Right* Bo Hoang Lam uses his moped to travel between the vast ponds at the prawn farm owned by Nguyen Thi Sam in Vietnam. *Top right* Washing down the deck at sunrise after a night's line fishing for tuna off the coast of Sri Lanka at Beruwala.

Asian shores

The seas around southeast Asia have long produced bountiful supplies of seafood for the people of the region. In these usually calm, turquoise waters, fishermen have plied their trade for centuries, bringing to shore seafood to be cooked into fragrant stews laced with coconut, or chargrilled on wood stoves. Today, Young's buys several species from this plentiful harvest – to be enjoyed all year round in the cooler climes of the UK.

Stir-fried salt & pepper squid with red chilli & spring onion

COURTESY OF RICK STEIN, THE SEAFOOD RESTAURANT

Preparation and cooking time 30 minutes

Rick Stein

Rick Stein runs four restaurants, a delicatessen, a patisserie, a seafood cookery school and a hotel in the small fishing port of Padstow in Cornwall. His Seafood Restaurant is booked for many months in advance and he attributes the success of all his ventures to a simple observation: "Nothing is more exhilarating than fresh fish simply cooked."

He has written nine cookery books and is a firm patron of the Marine Stewardship Council. Rick is also very interested in diet, particularly in the healthy properties of fish eaten at least twice a week, as it becomes more and more apparent with the increasing reports about Omega 3 that what our grandmothers told us is true – fish is good for the brain!

You will need

750g (1¹/₂ lb) squid
¹/₂ tsp black peppercorns
¹/₂ tsp Sichuan peppercorns
1 tsp Maldon sea-salt flakes
1–2 tbsp sunflower oil
1 medium-hot red Dutch chilli, thinly sliced (seeds removed, if you prefer)
3 spring onions, sliced

and for the salad

¹/₄ cucumber, peeled, halved and seeded
50g (2 oz) beansprouts
25g (1 oz) watercress, large stalks removed
2 tsp dark soy sauce
2 tsp roasted sesame oil
¹/₄ tsp caster sugar
a pinch of salt

1   Clean the squid and then cut along one side of each squid pouch and open it out flat. Score the inner side in a diamond pattern with the tip of a small, sharp knife, then cut into 5cm (2 inch) squares. Separate the tentacles if large.

2   For the salad, cut the cucumber lengthways into short strips. Toss with the beansprouts and watercress and set aside in the fridge until needed. Whisk together the soy sauce, sesame oil, sugar and salt.

3   Heat a small heavy-based frying pan over a high heat. Add the black peppercorns and Sichuan peppercorns and dry-roast them for a few seconds, shaking the pan now and then, until they darken slightly and become aromatic. Tip into a mortar and crush with the pestle, then stir in the sea-salt flakes.

4   Heat a wok over a high heat until smoking. Add half the oil and half the squid and stir-fry it for 2 minutes until lightly coloured. Tip on to a plate, and then cook the remaining squid in the same way.

5   Return the first batch of squid to the wok and add 1 tsp of the salt-and-pepper mixture (the rest can be used in other stir-fries). Toss together for about 10 seconds, then add the red chilli and spring onions and toss together very briefly.

6   Divide the squid between 4 serving plates. Toss the salad with the dressing and pile alongside the squid. Serve immediately.

Tuna from
Sri Lanka

Tuna is one of the staple industries of Sri Lanka, where it is still caught by the traditional line-caught method, the most environmentally friendly way of catching this large game-fish without damaging other ocean species. In 1995, the Ray brothers, Peter and David (originally from Kent) set up Apollo Marine, a company specialising in the fishing and export of yellow-fin tuna to the world market. Young's has worked with Apollo Marine since the start and the two companies have an excellent relationship – so much so that they were able to work closely together to put funds into assisting the restructuring of the local tuna-fishing community after the tsunami of December 2004.

Large image and below centre Fishermen weigh the large yellow fin tuna they have just caught. Bottom left Taking time out to eat lunch prepared by the skipper during a five-day tuna fishing trip. Bottom right One of the members of the six strong team that fish the Indian Ocean catching yellow fin tuna.

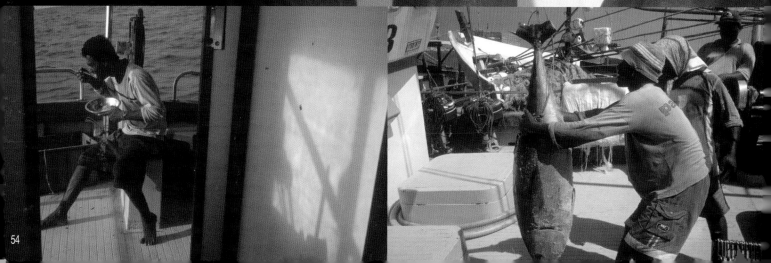

Tuna with sun-blush tomato & spring onion couscous

Serves 4

Preparation and cooking time 20 minutes

You will need

4 tuna steaks, weighing approx.
  115g (4 oz) each
1 tbsp olive oil
salt and freshly ground black
  pepper
200g (7 oz) natural yoghurt
1/2 tsp ground cumin

for the couscous

400g (14 oz) couscous
200g (7 oz) sun-blush
  tomatoes
6 tbsp extra virgin olive oil
juice of 1 lemon
bunch spring onions, finely
  sliced
2 tbsp chopped fresh
  parsley

1   First prepare the couscous by placing it in a bowl with the tomatoes and the extra virgin olive oil. Stir well, then pour over enough boiling water to cover. Leave to stand for 5 minutes.

2   Whisk the couscous around with a fork to loosen it. Add the lemon juice, spring onions, parsley and seasoning, stir gently and check for seasoning.

3   Heat the tablespoon of olive oil in a frying pan. Season the tuna steaks with salt and pepper and, when the oil is hot, fry over a high heat until cooked to your liking: 1–2 minutes each side for rare, 2–3 for medium.

4   Stir the cumin into the yoghurt.

5   Serve the tuna on a bed of couscous with a dollop of spicy yoghurt on the side.

If you like a really meaty fish, tuna steaks are great, plus they can be slapped on a barbecue, under the grill or on a griddle-pan and cooked in minutes.

Fishfact

Fresh tuna, which is dark red in colour, is usually available as meaty loins or steaks – these are perfect for barbecuing or serving just lightly seared, as in this recipe. You may also find tuna served raw as sashimi or sushi.

Seared tuna with tabbouleh & chilli oil

CLAIRE RANKIN

Serves 4

Preparation and cooking time **40 minutes**

For the tabbouleh

200g (7 oz) couscous
300ml (10 fl oz) chicken stock
1 chilli, deseeded and finely chopped
3 tbsp freshly chopped mint
3 tbsp freshly chopped parsley
3 tbsp freshly chopped coriander
100g (3¹/₂ oz) dates or sultanas, chopped
juice and grated zest of 1 lemon

for the chilli oil

100ml (3¹/₂ fl oz) olive oil
2 whole chillies, cut up roughly
1 clove garlic

and for the fish

4 tuna steaks
6 tbsp olive oil
2 cloves garlic, crushed
salt and freshly ground black pepper

1   Warm up a little olive oil in a pan and fry the chilli and garlic until soft. Add the rest of the oil and heat up, but do not boil. Leave to cool and place in a vinaigrette bottle with the chilli inside.

2   Bring the stock to the boil. Pour the couscous into a large bowl and slowly pour in the stock a little at a time fluffing it up with a fork. Do this until it cannot take any more liquid and then cover with clingfilm to keep in the heat. When it is all fluffed up add the remaining ingredients and season to taste.

3   Place the tuna in a non-metallic bowl. Pour over the olive oil and sprinkle with garlic and seasoning – leave to marinate for 10 minutes.

4   Heat a griddle-pan, wipe the tuna steaks with kitchen paper to take off the excess oil and season. Place the steaks on the griddle and cook for about 3 minutes on each side, depending on how rare you like your tuna.

5   To serve each individual plate, spoon the tabbouleh into a ramekin dish, press down and then turn out onto the plate. Rest the tuna on the tabbouleh and drizzle with chilli oil.

Alternative: Most white fish fillets can be cooked this way.

Claire Rankin

This recipe is by Claire Rankin, formerly chef at the 'Fish!' chain of stylish seafood restaurants. Claire is also an experienced radio and television broadcaster on food.

The devastating tsunami that hit the Indian Ocean in December 2004 affected many people who relied on fishing for their income and way of life. Since that time, Young's has continued to work closely with the Ray brothers, contributing money and support to help their tuna-fishing families to get back on their feet. New boats and fishing gear have been bought for those who lost them, and new land was purchased further inland, where homes for 16 families have been built, close to Beruwala town.

Even more important for this community than funds was Young's continued commitment to buy the tuna they catch, facilitating a faster economic recovery that can be sustained for the long term.

Recovering from the
tsunami

Raymond Blanc

All the clean, fresh flavours of Provence can be found in this fragrant dish. The obvious time to eat it is in the summer, when the tomatoes are fat and bursting with juices and sweetness and all the vegetables can be found locally and are packed with flavour. The ratatouille can be prepared up to a day ahead and the tomato coulis a few hours in advance.

Pan-fried fillet of sea bream with ratatouille & tomato coulis

RAYMOND BLANC

Preparation and cooking time 30 minutes

2 onions, cut into 2cm dice
4 sprigs of fresh thyme
4 tbsp olive oil
4 cloves garlic, crushed
2 large red peppers, deseeded and cut into 2cm dice
2 large courgettes, cut in half lengthways and cut into 2cm dice
1 medium aubergine, cut in half lengthways and cut into 2cm dice
2 tbsp tomato purée
4 plum tomatoes, chopped
sea salt and freshly ground black pepper

200g (7 oz) very ripe cherry tomatoes
2 tbsp extra virgin olive oil
2 pinches of sugar (if the tomatoes aren't ripe enough)
sea salt and freshly ground black pepper

4 sea bream fillets, descaled
1 tbsp extra virgin olive oil, plus extra for drizzling
juice of 1 lemon
sea salt and freshly ground black pepper

1   Pre-heat the oven to 200°C/400°F/Gas Mark 6.

2   On a medium heat, in a large saucepan, soften the onions and thyme in the olive oil for 3–4 minutes, without letting them colour. Add the garlic, red peppers, courgettes, aubergine, 8 pinches of salt and 4 pinches of pepper and cook for 2 minutes longer.

3   Stir in the tomato purée and chopped tomatoes. Cook over a medium heat, with a lid on, for 15–20 minutes, until the vegetables are tender. Taste and correct the seasoning if necessary, then set aside.

4   In a blender, or with a hand-held blender, purée the cherry tomatoes with the extra-virgin olive oil, 2 pinches of salt and a pinch of pepper. Taste and add the sugar if necessary, then strain and set aside.

5   Slash each fillet 3 times with a sharp knife (this allows the heat to penetrate more easily). Season with 4 pinches of salt and 2 of pepper. Over a high heat, in a large, oven-proof frying pan, heat the oil. Sear the fillets on the flesh side for 30–40 seconds in the hot olive oil. Turn the fillets over and cook for 2 – 3 minutes. Transfer to the oven and cook for 2–3 minutes longer, depending on thickness. Taste and correct the seasoning, if necessary, then sprinkle the lemon juice over the fillets.

6   To finish the dish reheat the ratatouille and gently warm the tomato coulis, making sure it does not boil (if it did it would become grainy and lose all its freshness). Arrange the ratatouille in the middle of 4 soup plates and top with the sea bream fillets. Spoon the tomato coulis around and then drizzle with the best extra-virgin olive oil.

GrahamCharlton

'The man from Young's'

Below Mr Thuan, sales and marketing director of the Truc Anh Corporation in Na Trang, Vietnam, sporting one of Graham's regular gifts to his suppliers – a Grimsby Town football shirt!

The buyer's story

Graham Charlton has spent 40 years in the seafood industry. He joined Young's in Grimsby as a raw recruit – becoming a trainee fish-buyer straight from school in April 1965 at the age of 15.

Graham then moved through purchasing to production and factory management, but always with an emphasis on buying fish. His working life involved many very early mornings at the fish market and trips to European ports, gaining an in-depth understanding of the landing, grading and auctioning of various species.

As time moved on, so his expertise and experience broadened. In the 1980s, Graham was agreeing contracts in the northern Baltic for thousands of tonnes of cod a year, and soon found that the search for new kinds of fish was taking him to some amazing places.

"Twenty years ago, the market started to develop and I began travelling further to find the new species that supermarkets were demanding. In those days Spain and Florida seemed exotic, but the past ten years have led me much further afield!"

After the formation of Young's Bluecrest in 1999, the drive for new species quickened and Graham has been heavily involved in helping the company seek out the very best fish the world has to offer. He estimates that he has now visited more than 30 countries, seen a vast number of airports and travelled on every form of transport – from speedboat to bicycle!

"These recent years have been so exciting," says Graham. "One of Young's most important roles is to be a bridge between ordinary shoppers and the world's most fantastic seafood. So I now travel to places like Vietnam, Colombia and El Salvador, looking for delicious fish like new species of prawns, which are just becoming really popular in the UK. Life is never ever dull, I have met some fascinating people and made good friends with suppliers in far-flung places, which somehow makes the world seem a smaller place."

So, what will Graham do when he finally retires? "Well, actually, do some more travelling! We will be taking the grandchildren abroad and there are a good number of countries still to see!"

Amongst the mangroves

In Colombia, south American fishermen nose their boats through waters fringed by mangrove swamps. Here is where you find the new industry of prawn farming, which has to be carefully conducted so as not to destroy the fragile ecosystem. Young's has chosen its suppliers sensitively in Colombia, working only with farmers who know how to work carefully in this beautiful land, keeping their natural environment safe.

Opposite The sun sets on the beautiful landscape around the Cartagena Shrimp Company's farm in Colombia.
Top right A view of the Cartagena Shrimp Farm.
Above Checking the mangrove areas around the farms is part of the management of the local landscape.
Left Workers feed shrimp by hand in one of the many ponds at the Cartagena Shrimp Company Farm.

Prawns
from Colombia

There is a growing British appetite for shellfish and in particular the large, succulent *Penaeus* species of warm-water prawns. Young's buys warm water prawns from a number of suppliers in both Latin America and the Far East, particularly the species *Penaeus vannamei* – commonly known as Pacific white prawns or shrimp. One major source is the Cartagena Shrimp Company, which is based near Cartagena de Indias, in Colombia.

Cartagena is a highly respected operation that rears shrimp from its own hatchery. The company is noted for its high environmental standards, particularly the management of water in its farm and hatchery and the protection of the large mangrove swamps around its farms.

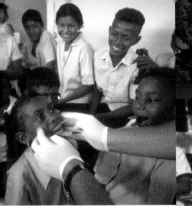

Top left Feeding shrimp in the ponds.
Bottom left One of the workers at Cartagena.
Above Schoolchildren receiving free health checks at school.
Top right Children and teachers enjoy the grounds of the new school, which was set up and funded by the Cartagena Shrimp Company.
Bottom right At the start of the new school year, one pupil poses proudly in the school's newly designed uniform.

Exporting top quality prawns to the UK has brought new prosperity to the Colombian shrimp farmers. In particular, working with Young's has helped the Cartagena Shrimp Company to improve its existing community projects, such as building a new school for local families and ensuring free health care for the children.

Fragrant green curry with prawns

A favourite with anybody who likes exotic food, here is a creamy coconut curry with succulent warm-water prawns, such as those sourced by Young's from both Vietnam and Colombia.

Serves 4

Preparation and cooking time 35 minutes

You will need

- 1 tbsp olive oil
- 1 onion, peeled and sliced
- 1 red pepper, deseeded and sliced
- 3 tsp green Thai curry paste
- 1 x 400ml can coconut milk
- 110g (3¾ oz) broccoli florets
- 135g (4¾ oz) cauliflower florets
- 75g (2¾ oz) mangetout
- 250g (9 oz) raw tiger prawns, peeled
- 1 tbsp freshly chopped basil
- 2 tbsp freshly chopped coriander
- salt and freshly ground black pepper

1. Heat the oil in a wok or large frying pan and stir-fry the onion and red pepper for 2–3 minutes.
2. Stir in the green Thai curry paste and pour in the coconut milk – cook for 1 minute.
3. Add the remaining vegetables, stir well and simmer for 8–10 minutes.
4. Stir in the prawns and cook for a further 2–3 minutes until the prawns are cooked through.
5. Check the seasoning and stir in the chopped basil and coriander. Serve hot with Thai fragrant rice.

Fishfact Just as in the rest of the world, prawns are among the UK's favourite seafoods. Worldwide, more than 50 species are sold regularly, and farming in tropical countries now provides over a third of global production.

Stateside

Seattle, on the west coast of the USA, where the Pacific Ocean seems to stretch out to infinity. Sea fishing has a long and hardy tradition here. Trawlers turn their back on the mild climate and enter the wild, icy seas of Alaska in search of salmon, cod and pollock. The battered vessels return days later laden with their cargo of silver muscular fish.

Left President and CEO Chuck Bundrant, aboard one of his fleet in Seattle, USA. *Large image* Seattle fisherman and boat-repairer Roy Wagner. *Below* Fishing amongst the glaciers in Alaska; and wild Pacific salmon at Seattle market.

Roasted salmon with salsa picante & coriander

MITCHELL TONKS

This simple recipe from Mitch Tonks is delicious made with wild Pacific salmon.

You will need

handful of pumpkin seeds
1 tsp sesame seeds
1 tsp cumin seeds
4 roasted tomatoes
6 tbsp cider vinegar
handful of fresh coriander
juice of 1 lime

3 whole hot chillies, seeds removed
1 tbsp dried oregano
4 cloves of garlic
4 pieces of salmon fillet weighing about 150g each

1   Make the salsa by toasting the seeds until golden in a heavy-based frying pan. Add to a food processor and then pile in all the other ingredients except the salmon. Whizz, making sure that you don't overdo it – you need a roughly chopped feel.

2   Sear the salmon in a hot pan until golden and then finish cooking in a hot oven for a further 4–5 minutes until just pink on the inside. Serve with a spoonful of the sauce, a wedge of lime and a sprig of coriander.

Fishfact Did you know that a fully grown female cod spawns up to 9 million eggs every year?

Wild Pacific salmon and Alaskan pollock, North America

Young's buys many of its staple fish species, such as Pacific salmon and Alaskan pollock, from suppliers who fish way up in cold northern waters, such as Trident Seafoods and American Seafoods – both based in Seattle. They fish from sustainable fisheries in the waters off Alaska and the North Pacific, where cold, rich ocean currents sustain large stocks of fish such as Pacific salmon, Alaskan pollock. Pacific cod and white halibut.

The pollock fishery in the Gulf of Alaska was certified by the Marine Stewardship Council as sustainable in April 2005.

Oysters Rockefeller

Preparation and cooking time **15 minutes**

You will need

1kg (2 lb) fresh spinach, washed
24 oysters, opened, with juice reserved
50g (1³/₄ oz) butter
100g (3¹/₂ oz) shallots, finely chopped
3 cloves garlic, crushed
2 tbsp thick double cream
2 tbsp Pernod
pinch chilli flakes
100g (3¹/₂ oz) Gruyere cheese, grated
salt and freshly ground black pepper

1   Place the washed spinach in a large saucepan with 1 tbsp water. Heat gently for 3–4 minutes until just wilted, drain and squeeze out any excess liquid. Chop finely.

2   Arrange the oysters in a baking dish. Melt the butter and sauté the shallots and garlic. Stir in the spinach, oyster juice and seasoning.

3   Add the cream and bring to a simmer for 1–2 minutes. Purée the mixture in a food processor or blender and return to a clean pan.

4   Add the Pernod and chilli flakes and heat gently until warm.

5   Spoon the mixture over each oyster and then sprinkle with cheese. Place under a hot grill until the cheese sizzles.

Oysters have always been linked with love and are reputed to be good for your sex life! One thing is for sure, they contain enough vitamins and minerals for a healthy meal alone and with only 75 calories for 12 oysters you don't even have to worry about your weight! Always buy oysters from a reputable fishmonger to ensure freshness. If you are unsure about eating raw oysters, this recipe is perfect.

Fishfact A live and really fresh oyster uses the top and bottom muscles to hold the shell securely closed. If oysters are not fresh the shell will be open slightly – these are not to be eaten!

Crayfish linguini with cherry tomatoes & rocket

Serves 4

Preparation and cooking time 20 minutes

You will need

400g (14 oz) cooked crayfish tails
500g (1 lb 2 oz) dried linguini
4 tbsp extra virgin olive oil
2 cloves garlic, finely chopped
1 tsp dried chilli flakes

150g (5$^{1}/_{2}$ oz) cherry tomatoes, halved
100ml (3$^{1}/_{2}$ fl oz) dry white wine
2 tbsp freshly chopped parsley
150g (5$^{1}/_{2}$ oz) rocket
salt and freshly ground black pepper

1 Cook the linguini in a large pan of boiling salted water, until al dente.

2 Meanwhile heat the olive oil in a frying pan, add the garlic, chilli and tomatoes and cook gently for a couple of minutes.

3 Add the crayfish tails and white wine and cook for a couple of minutes to reduce the wine.

4 Drain the linguini and add to the frying pan. Toss to combine and season well.

5 Divide the rocket between four pasta bowls or plates and serve the crayfish and linguini on top – the heat from the pasta will wilt the rocket without over cooking it.

Alternative: Cray can be substituted with cooked lobster or prawns if wished.

Confusingly, there are freshwater or seawater crayfish, and seawater crayfish can also be called crawfish or rock lobster. If you happen to be in Louisiana, USA, crawfish are freshwater crayfish! The difference is in the length – freshwater crayfish are quite small, about 8–10cm long, whereas rock lobsters are much larger.

Fishtip Undercooking rather than overcooking is the key to crayfish – if they are cooked too long they become quite chewy.

The health benefits of fish

"*Eat fish!*" you say.

"*Why?*" I say.

"*Because it's good for you!*" you say.

"*Who says?*" I say.

"*The government and a whole load of scientists!*" you say.

In fact, fish is so good for you the Food Standards Agency now recommends we all eat it twice a week. Are you getting yours?

Fishfact For an easy and delicious way to enjoy fish rich in Omega 3, try a Young's salmon product or look out for the 'Young's at Heart' logo on packs at your local supermarket.

Fish and fats

- The body needs a recommended amount of both saturated and unsaturated fats per day.
- Exceeding the recommendation can cause health problems associated with being overweight, but not fulfilling the recommendation can also lead to other health problems!
- The UK population has a diet far too high in saturated fat and eating fish is an effective way of controlling fat and the 'type of fat' intake.
- Oily fish species are high in essential Omega 3 polyunsaturated fats which are proven to help maintain a healthy heart.
- White fish is particularly low in fat – eating more of it can help keep your fat intake to the recommended government levels.

Are you getting enough?

- Fish is a good way of keeping a balanced diet. Apart from the health benefits outlined above, fish is also particularly rich in Vitamins B and D, zinc, phosphorus, calcium and iron.
- To fulfil these health benefits, the government recommends we eat one portion of oily fish and one portion of white fish per week. UK consumers currently eat 25% of the oily fish and 50% of the white fish recommendation.

Everyone knows fish is good for kids. But why?

- Omega 3 is vital for the functional development of the child from unborn baby until post-teenage years – improving memory, learning ability, eyesight, teeth, skin and bone strength.
- White fish is also good for lowering the fat intake of today's children. In a world where those under 18 are less active and more obese than those over 65, fish is an excellent option, tasty and low in saturated fat.

Fish gives you energy

- The Omega 3 contained in oily fish provides the vast majority of the brain's energy. It also balances out the production of depressants that make you lethargic – keeping you full of energy.
- White fish can also stimulate the body's energy as it contains high levels of iodine and niacin.

Fish makes you brainy

- How? By improving your learning power and memory!
- Most white fish is a good source of zinc, which improves mental functioning and memory.
- The Omega 3 in oily fish provides most of the energy for the brain – improving your learning power and mental functioning.
- Omega 3 also makes you happy, stimulates your 'happy chemicals' and wards off headaches!

Oily fish are **amazing!**

Your two portions of fish a week should include at least one of an oily fish such as salmon, mackerel or herring. These fish are rich in Omega 3, a natural oil proven in dozens of studies to have amazing health benefits – from helping with heart disease, asthma and Alzheimer's to boosting the brain power of kids! Oxford Professor John Stein (brother of Rick) is an Omega 3 advocate – he has found it helps patients with dyslexia.

The earliest anecdotal evidence for the benefits of Omega 3 came from observations of the long life and virtual absence of heart disease seen among peoples with a high-fish diet such as the Danish, Inuit and many Mediterranean peoples. So initial research about Omega 3 related mainly to the way it helped combat heart disease, but dozens of studies since then have shown that Omega 3 can make a vital contribution to health at every stage of human life.

Find out more about the health benefits of oily fish at www.richinomega3.com

Roasted sardines

ROSE GRAY & RUTH ROGERS

Serves 4 as a starter

Preparation and cooking time **10-15 minutes**

Rose Gray & Ruth Rogers
Rose Gray and Ruth Rogers, founders of the renowned River Cafe, are famous for their innovative approach to food.

Taken from their book, *River Café Cook Book Easy* this is a deliciously quick and easy way to enjoy fresh sardines, oily fish which are packed with Omega 3 and extremely good for you!

You will need

24 sardines
500g cherry tomatoes
extra virgin olive oil
50g black olilves
4 lemons

1 Pierce the tomatoes with a fork. Toss with olive oil, season and bake for 15 minutes.

2 Stone the olives and grate the peel of two lemons. Use an ovenproof dish large enough to hold all the sardines in one layer, then drizzle with olive oil. Place the sardines in, side by side and season. Sprinkle over the lemon zest, olives and tomatoes and drizzle with olive oil. Bake for 10 minutes. Serve with lemon.

Fishtip Eating a whole cooked Fish

Peel the skin away from the flesh. Cut down to the backbone along the lateral line. Slide the flat of the knife underneath the flesh and lift away the first half of the segment. Repeat for the remaining part of the segment opposite and for the rest of the first side of the fish. Lift away the skeleton to reveal the side of the fish remaining underneath.

Cooking up something delicious

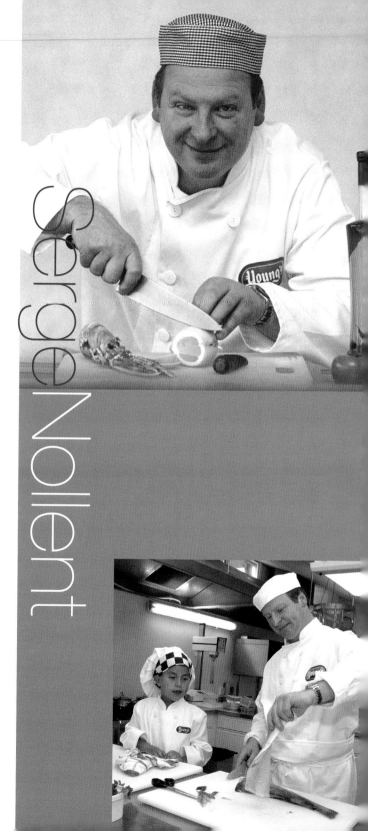

Serge Nollent

With 25 years' experience, Serge Nollent is Young's senior development chef. Born in Beuzeville – a small village in Normandy – he started French chef school at the age of 14! "I was brought up in a farming family with a love of fresh produce," he says. "My mum in particular was a big influence on me, from an early age she had me making black pudding and other delicacies. Then when I was 12, I got a summer job in a restaurant and after that I was hooked!"

After his training, Serge got his first chef's job at the renowned Normandy Hotel in Deauville, in a kitchen of 35 chefs! He then spent a number of years travelling, broadening his horizons in places such as Germany, at Klosters in Switzerland and Bergen in Norway. He also spent more time in France undertaking the traditional chefs' 'Tour' – working around the country to build up particular regional skills.

Serge's cosmopolitan outlook and desire to find out more about food eventually led him to Scotland, where he worked firstly in Oban and then, in St Andrews, became the youngest head chef in Scotland at the age of 22. He also discovered the joys of Scottish seafood. "I particularly enjoyed going to the market at Crail and buying fantastic fresh langoustines for the restaurant."

Also in St Andrews, Serge met his future wife and started putting down roots in the UK. The couple moved to Yorkshire, where he helped set up a new restaurant in Huddersfield. "Our backer was a wealthy Yorkshire businessman who called the restaurant 'Pisces' after his daughter's star sign!" The restaurant was a big hit and soon was listed in the Good Food Guide.

So, why did Serge change his horizons to the development kitchen? "Well, I saw a job advertised and a friend suggested I try for it. After a number of years with other food producers, I eventually joined Young's in 1999.

"We have a great team here – it's lots of fun and certainly never dull. For me, working in development really means you can have a bigger impact. I find it fantastically rewarding to know that something you have created ends up not just on a few people's plates, but becomes a dish that will be enjoyed by thousands!"

Coquille Saint Jacques with champagne & creamed leek

SERGE NOLLENT

Serge says, "There are so many different ways to cook fish and it's always easier than you think. If you fancy something a little different, why not try my favourite recipe for scallops? I am sure your guests will be most impressed!"

Serves 4

Preparation and cooking time **40 minutes**

You will need

100g (3½ oz) butter	1 leek, sliced
1 shallot, thinly sliced	16 king large sea scallops
225ml (8 fl oz) fish stock	110ml (3¾ fl oz) champagne
200ml (7 fl oz) double cream	juice of ½ lemon
salt and freshly ground black pepper	1 tsp chopped chives

Coquille St Jacques is also available ready prepared from Young's – one of a delicious range of new chilled starter dishes.

1   Melt 80g (3 oz) of the butter in a small pan, add the shallot and cook for 3–4 minutes until soft.

2   Add the fish stock, bring to the boil and reduce by half. Add 120ml (3¾ fl oz) double cream, bring to the boil again then reduce to a simmer and cook for 10 minutes. Strain the sauce, taste for seasoning and keep warm.

3   Melt a knob of butter in a pan and sweat the leek for about 2 minutes. Add the remaining cream and cook for 5 minutes. Keep warm.

4   Pat the scallops dry and season them. Heat the remaining butter in a sauté pan over a high heat. Once the butter starts to foam add the scallops. Cook on one side for about 3 minutes and then repeat on the other side. Remove from the pan and keep warm.

5   Discard the excess fat from the sauté pan, return to the heat and pour in the champagne, scraping the pan with a wooden spoon. Bring to the boil and reduce by three-quarters.

6   Add the creamy shallot mixture, remove from the heat and stir in the lemon juice and chives.

7   Arrange the scallops on a serving platter, place the creamed leek in the middle and pour over the sauce.

Index of recipes